WAY TO GROW! GARDENING
VEGETABLES

by Rebecca Pettiford

pogo

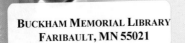

Ideas for Parents and Teachers

Pogo Books let children practice reading informational text while introducing them to nonfiction features such as headings, labels, sidebars, maps, and diagrams, as well as a table of contents, glossary, and index.

Carefully leveled text with a strong photo match offers early fluent readers the support they need to succeed.

Before Reading

- "Walk" through the book and point out the various nonfiction features. Ask the student what purpose each feature serves.
- Look at the glossary together. Read and discuss the words.

Read the Book

- Have the child read the book independently.
- Invite him or her to list questions that arise from reading.

After Reading

- Discuss the child's questions. Talk about how he or she might find answers to those questions.
- Prompt the child to think more. Ask: What is your favorite vegetable? Does it grow underground or aboveground? Have you ever grown it yourself?

Pogo Books are published by Jump!
5357 Penn Avenue South
Minneapolis, MN 55419
www.jumplibrary.com

Library of Congress Cataloging-in-Publication Data

Pettiford, Rebecca, author.
  Vegetables / by Rebecca Pettiford.
     pages cm. – (Way to grow! Gardening)
  Includes index.
  ISBN 978-1-62031-233-9 (hardcover: alk. paper) –
  ISBN 978-1-62496-320-9 (ebook)
  1. Vegetable gardening–Juvenile literature.
  2. Vegetables–Juvenile literature. I. Title. II. Series: Pettiford, Rebecca. Way to grow! Gardening.
  SB324.P48 2015
  635–dc23
                                    2015000296

Series Editor: Jenny Fretland VanVoorst
Series Designer: Anna Peterson
Photo Researcher: Anna Peterson

Photo Credits: All photos by Thinkstock except: Getty, 5, 6-7, 12-13, 18-19, 21; iStock, cover; Shutterstock, 4, 8-9, 20, 23.

Printed in the United States of America at Corporate Graphics in North Mankato, Minnesota.

TABLE OF CONTENTS

CHAPTER 1

PLANTING A VEGETABLE GARDEN

Vegetables may not be your favorite things to eat. But that just means you've never had them fresh from your own garden.

Growing your own vegetables is fun and delicious. It's good for you and the earth, too.

Many vegetables are easy to grow. Let's learn how!

seedling

Most vegetables are **annuals**. You plant them every year. If you plant seeds, you can start them inside. You can plant **seedlings** in the ground after the last frost in March or April.

There are many different vegetables. **Root vegetables**, like carrots and onions, grow under the ground. **Leafy vegetables**, like lettuce and spinach, grow above the ground.

DID YOU KNOW?

Many foods we think of as vegetables are actually fruits. Fruits contain the plant's seeds. Squash, tomatoes, and peppers are fruits. But because they are not sweet, they are usually counted as vegetables.

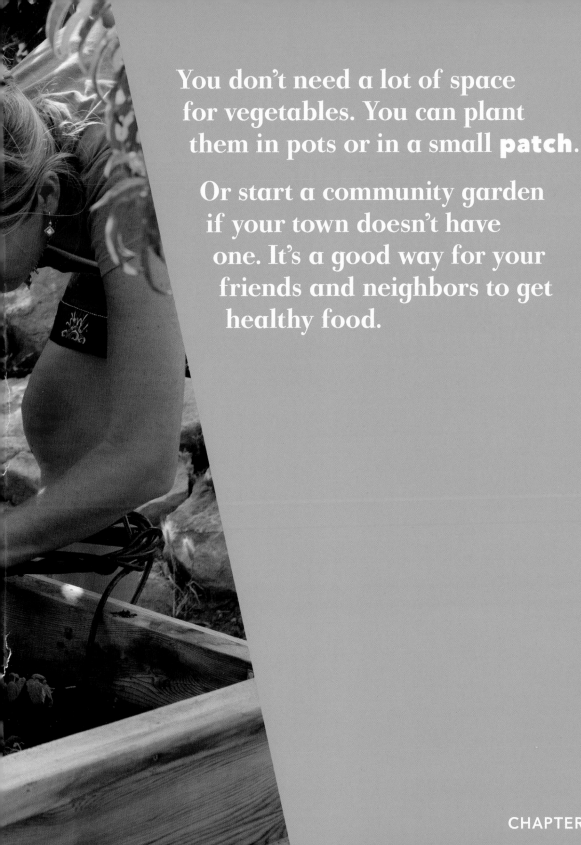

You don't need a lot of space for vegetables. You can plant them in pots or in a small **patch**.

Or start a community garden if your town doesn't have one. It's a good way for your friends and neighbors to get healthy food.

To make sure your garden is a success, you need good soil. Vegetables like well-drained soil that is rich in **organic matter**. Add **compost** and **manure** to your soil. The soil needs to be loose before you plant. Use a shovel or a garden fork to turn it.

organic
matter

A good way to make healthy soil is to use **raised beds**. The soil in the beds is higher than the ground. It never gets stepped on. It warms up faster in the spring. It drains faster in wet weather.

DID YOU KNOW?

Raised beds make it harder for snails and other pests to get to your plants.

raised bed

CHAPTER 2

CARING FOR YOUR GARDEN

Most vegetables need a lot of sun.

Water the plants early in the morning. If you water late in the day, the water could be quickly lost to the hot sun.

Some flowers and **herbs** have a strong odor. Many pests don't like them. If you plant them near your vegetables, you can help keep pests away.

DID YOU KNOW?

Many gardeners grow basil near their tomato plants. Basil is said to keep bugs away. Some also believe it improves the flavor of the tomatoes!

CHAPTER 3

HARVESTING VEGETABLES

Are your vegetables ready to pick? It depends.

You can gather some when they are ripe. You can pick others early. They will ripen inside.

If your vegetables look good enough to eat, they are ready!

ACTIVITIES & TOOLS

PLANT RADISH SEEDS

Radishes are one of the first vegetables to harvest in the spring. Start them inside, and soon you will have a crunchy treat. Here's how:

What You Need:
- a large pot
- a few stones
- compost
- radish seeds

1. Put a few stones in the bottom of a large pot. This lets water drain.

2. Fill your pot with compost. Put your radish seeds in the compost about one quarter inch (.6 centimeters) deep.

3. Put your pot in a sunny spot. Water your seeds whenever the compost seems dry.

4. Once your radishes begin to grow, take out some of the seedlings. Plant them outside about an inch (2.5 cm) apart. This gives them room to grow.

5. In about four weeks, your radishes will be ready to pick!

6. Enjoy them raw or sliced on a salad. Congratulations! You grew them yourself.

GLOSSARY

annuals: Vegetables that you plant every year.

compost: A rotted mix of leaves, grass, and paper that makes garden soil healthy.

herbs: Plants that add flavor to food or are used to make perfume and medicine.

leafy vegetables: Vegetables that grow above the ground.

manure: Bodily waste from farm animals like chickens and cows.

organic matter: The remains of plants and animals and their waste products.

patch: A small piece of ground used for gardening.

raised beds: Garden beds that are built above ground level.

root vegetables: Vegetables that grow under the ground.

seedlings: Young plants grown from seed.

INDEX

TO LEARN MORE

Learning more is as easy as 1, 2, 3.

1) Go to www.factsurfer.com

2) Enter "vegetables" into the search box.

3) Click the "Surf" to see a list of websites.

With factsurfer, finding more information is just a click away.